Bear Spotting

Written by Isabel Thomas

Contents

Collins

Look out!

There are bears about.
Each kind of bear has:
- a long snout
- small ears
- a short tail.

But bears are found in many different habitats, and eat many different kinds of foods.

Brown bear

This group of brown bears is fishing in a river in Alaska. They stand on boulders in the water and wait for fish to jump into their mouths!

Panda

Wild pandas are found
in China, where they eat
just one plant: bamboo.
Their paws have an extra
bone to help them
grasp bamboo shoots
and stems.

Polar bear

Polar bears are skilful swimmers. They roam the cold Arctic, hunting for animals like seals and sea birds to eat.

Moon bear

Moon bears
can be found in China,
Japan and
the Himalayas.
They munch nuts,
seeds, insects, birds
and even small animals
like mice.

11

Sloth bear

Sloth bears hang upside down from trees. Their front teeth are missing so they can suck up insects. Their nostrils seal shut to stop termites crawling in!

Sun bear

The world's smallest bear,
the sun bear, hides in rainforests.
Its sharp claws help it tear
open beehives to get at the
honey. Its powerful jaws can
crack coconuts!

American black bear

In North America, black bears visit meadows to eat grass and other plants. You might catch them eating scraps that humans have thrown away, too.

A bear with glasses!

South American bears have markings that look like glasses! They eat high up in trees. They sleep up there, too – they even make themselves a treehouse for sleeping in!

19

Under threat

Six of the bears in this book are rare and under threat. We can help bears by protecting their homes.

Spotting bears

Review: After reading

Use your assessment from hearing the children read to choose any GPCs, words or tricky words that need additional practice.

Read 1: Decoding

- Look at page 2 together and turn to the first sentence. Ask the children:
  - Can you find two words that rhyme? (*bear, there*)
  - For each word, can you point to the part of the word that represents the /air/ sound?
  - Can you think of other words that contain the /air/ sound? (e.g. *hair, care, pear*)
- You could now do the same thing for the /ow/ sound on page 4 (*brown, mouths*) or the /ee/ sound on page 18. (*sleeping, eat, trees*)

Read 2: Prosody

- Choose two double page spreads and model reading with expression to the children. Ask the children to have a go at reading the same pages with expression.
- Model reading a page of bear facts as if you are a nature documentary presenter. Use your voice to create interest. Ask the children to read a page in the same manner.

Read 3: Comprehension

- For every question ask the children how they know the answer. Ask:
  - Can you remember some of the different types of bears?
  - Which bear was your favourite? Why?
  - Did you find out what you had hoped to before you read this book?